My Mountain Country

Ye Lijun

叶丽隽

*Translated from the Chinese
by* Fiona Sze-Lorrain

Foreword by Christopher Merrill

WORLD POETRY BOOKS

World Poetry Books
Storrs, CT 06269
www.worldpoetrybooks.com
English translation copyright © 2019 by Fiona Sze-Lorrain
All rights reserved

This book is made possible with support from the Stavros Niarchos Foundation.

Library of Congress Cataloging-in-Publication Data
Names: Ye, Lijun, author; Sze-Lorrain, Fiona, translator
Title: My Mountain Country / Ye Lijun
Description: Storrs, Connecticut: World Poetry Books [2019]
Identifiers: LCCN 2019942280
    ISBN 978-0-9992613-4-7
Published in the United States of America
2 4 6 8 10 9 7 5 3 1
Cover design by Kyle G. Hunter
Book design by Brian Sneeden

CONTENTS

FOREWORD

"In this world dwells the joy of imagination," Ye Lijun
writes in a poem titled "The Secret Hour." And the joys revealed
in *My Mountain Country*, which brings together a selection
of poems from her three books, elegantly translated by Fiona
Sze-Lorrain, suggest that for an acute observer of the natural
world every hour, secret or not, may become an occasion for
opening, "in clarity," to the beloved, to nature, to the invisible—
leaves and roses and flowering trees that at a moment's notice
may awaken in her soul, alerting her once again to the mysteri-
ous bounty of life on earth. Ye Lijun is a remarkable poet, whose
timeless view of her place in the great chain of being could not
be more timely; for she knows how to savor what humankind
seems bent on destroying. If her poems offer what Robert Frost
called "a momentary stay against confusion," then it is the chaos
of climate change, air and water pollution, rampant develop-
ment, economic dislocation, and the complications of love and
loss that summon her formidable powers of attention, musical
gifts, wit, wisdom, and determination to explore the meaning of
our walk in the sun. To understand why we so often ruin what
sustains us, we might begin by reading Ye Lijun's poems.

Take, for example, "Song of Tremble," which presents
an altogether original vision of the relationship between the
human and nonhuman realms:

Devoured, like snow into sea
Even my alarmed cries can't stop you

You, this quiet
sea tyrant, brewing clamor of the flesh, between wave and wave

You lead me to disappearance
and restore me, again in this deep blue ... You are a child
so stubborn, seeking in my revived land
the origin of life

I feel so ashamed—O Lord
a life seems to begin
Disquiet is ambushed in the subtle bliss

Think of this as a message in a bottle, composed together by
Paul Celan and Tu Fu clinging to a piece of driftwood out
at sea, which Ye Lijun subsequently found on the beach and
translated for this age of apocalypse. What she discovers in
the "brewing clamor of the flesh, between wave and wave," in a
language that is by turns biblical, plain-spoken, and unnerving,
is the sudden way in which bliss can be undone in a flash—of
insight, accident, or error. What will revive us? No one knows.
But this poet has an uncanny ability to map that strange land
hidden within us all.

The house described in "Whereabouts," in which Ye Lijun cultivated the art of solitude as a form of meditation on the changing landscape of her childhood home, is subject to the passage of time and the encroachments of nature: two constants in her work. And this: "A mountain. Down the mountain / a tunnel, sometimes echoes of singing late at night." The songs of lamentation that Ye Lijun hears in that tunnel, faithfully transcribes, and then adapts for the calamitous days and nights that lie before us will echo for a very long time to come. Listen closely.

Christopher Merrill

My Mountain Country

坐等天明

关上窗也能听到，屋后的山上
涛声如雨。我似乎睡过
在林子摇晃之前
被窗下的蛐蛐声带远

外面，树木和小兽们
漫过了月光下的栅栏，喧嚣着
蜂拥至我心的边缘……可我
身无长物，不比任何一棵树木，拥有得更多

甚至，一棵草。我只是
抱紧了自己，坐在这黑暗、晃动的中心
屏息聆听，直到

这世界奏响了它的最高音阶
——黎明，一片寂静。我便也选择了
喑哑不语

Sitting and Waiting for Daybreak

Even with windows shut one can hear, on the mountain behind the house
waves like rain. I seem to have slept
before the woods waver
carried afar by crickets' chirping under the window

Outside, trees and little beasts
surge over railings under the moonlight, in a clamor
bees swarm to the edge of my heart . . . But I
am poor, own no more than any plant does

no more than even a strand of grass. I just
hug myself, sit in this dim, wobbly center
listen with breath held, until

this world sounds its highest scale
—dawn, stillness. And I choose
to utter no word

SONG OF TREMBLE

秘密的时辰

打开我。不管另一边是什么
我的生硬、枯涩
我身上，所有遭受腐蚀的迹象
等待着被抚摩，被穿过
等待着洞然而开，通往这个特定的时刻
通往你。当我夜里醒来，睁着眼，和恐惧一起躺在黑暗里
看不见的事物哗哗流逝
唯有你啊，越来越清晰
你是我的。是我的。这世间有想象中获得的快乐
我绿叶丛生
我蔷薇萌动
我就这样占有了我所没有的东西
一支幻想的军队

The Secret Hour

Open me. No matter what lies on the other side
my rigidity and dullness
signs on my body suffering from corrosion
wait to be fondled, to be pierced
wait to open in clarity, leading to this specific instant
and you. Roused at night, eyes wide open, I lie with fear in darkness
all invisibles fade in a rush
Save for you, clearer tint by tint
You are mine. Mine. In this world dwells the joy of imagination
I cluster leaves
I awaken roses
Just like this, I possess what I don't
An imaginary troop

裸春

冲澡后，不急着穿衣
在这个阳光明媚的房间里
一无牵挂地走动
翻书、喝茶、翘着脚小憩
看时光金黄的豹子
随午后的流逝，沿着大腿
慢慢爬上我的腹部
窗外，是片光秃的树林子
一根根赤裸的枝条
萌动着多少青葱的欲求
我知道对面的楼宇中
一定也有我这样
临窗的人
但我并没有感到丝毫的不安
我甚至打开了这空调间的窗户，让那
刮过每根枝条的风
也都刮到我的身上来
已经是三月。春天了，有什么
是不可以的呢

Naked Spring

No rush to dress after a shower
In this bright and splendid room
I walk around with no worries
flip through books, sip tea, rest with legs crossed
watching time, a golden leopard
Along my thighs, as the afternoon goes by
it slowly climbs onto my belly
Outside the window, a forest of bald trees
Naked branches one by one
How many green desires do they sprout
I know in the opposite building
there must also be someone
like me by the window
But I have no qualms
I even open the window in this air-conditioned room, let
the wind scraping past each branch
blow against my body
Already March. Spring is here, what
isn't possible

不觉晓

当她说出
那一定是另外的星图。所以
原谅这个枯坐的人
原谅她的缄默、混沌和轻狂
以及新生儿般的无知
漫漫长夜
原谅她的无法停止
她靠着记忆中那毁灭与废墟的能量生活
也靠着一些瞬间
靠着那占据她心头的，像贝壳一样弯曲着的
内敛、缩小的
不可撤销的

Oblivion

Once spoken aloud
her words become a star chart of its own—
forgive her, a poet who sits through hours of idleness
forgive her silence, ignorance, impudence
her baby-like innocence
Long, endless night
forgive her for not slowing down
She lives on the force of wreckage in her memory
and fleeting instants
something on her mind, curved like a seashell
reserved, shrinking
irreversible

不惑图

临近中年的窗口
风景并未变得清晰
漆痕斑驳的画笔，滴落着时间
反观自身，我还是
那个无地自容的人哪
还是无法自如地描绘 ——
你好，午后的寂静、以及我
空空如也的胸怀
就让这一生，弯成一个问号吧
让草木归其泽
愤怒，也不要消失

Portrait at Forty

Close to middle age: the view
from my window, hardly clear
Paintbrush stained with paint drips of time
Introspection: I'm still
so ashamed and embarrassed
still can't portray myself with ease—
Hello, afternoon stillness, and my
empty chest
Just let this life curve into a question mark
Let luster return to nature
and fury, not disappear

树

我接受自己，以一种
与自己的尺寸成比例的方式
埋首于尘埃
有时候，甚至忽略了时序节令的推移
这没什么，我想
虽然不能返回，但是可以增加和繁殖
在我伸出的每根枝条上
都将继续怀着这些秘密：
积雪、小纸条、药丸、暗室中的亲吻、青屋里
寂寞盛开的茶花……
近乎于放纵，我四面八方地生长
在命运拥有我的地方
在我自身的界限里。那么当蓝星升起，谁
将豢养一颗狮子般的心呢

Tree

I embrace myself, in proportion
to my own dimensions
steeped in dust
Sometimes I even overlook the sequence of a season
No big deal, I suppose
Although I can't go back in time, I may grow and multiply
Each branch I extend
will carry on these secrets:
a heap of snow, paper slips, pills, kisses in the darkroom, lonely camellias
blossoming in my green brick house . . .
Close to indulgence, I grow far and near
where fate possesses me
within the limits of my own self. As blue stars rise, who
will feed a lion heart

就我记忆所及

你繁茂
高昂着，蔷薇花丛。你浓密的络腮胡子
柔韧的茎梗，痒痒地
戳着我的心。你的双眸里
有恣睢和纵容，一对追逐的流萤
永远闪烁在往事中
你紧绷的躯体，藤蔓一样
交叠在我腰间的双臂（那温暖，可以持续一生）
你胸腔的磁性音响，一个蜂巢
淡淡的生殖气息……我们仅有的一次慢三
是我赤着脚
踩在你宽大的脚背上
一二三、一二三
闭着眼，整个地埋首于你挺拔的枝干
我们旋转着，树叶纷披
绿色的，都是绿色的
没有别的事物在我们之间
说真的，最后你全身简直成了一个花园

Within the Reach of My Memory

You flourish
elated, among roses. Your bushy beard
like willowy stems, tickles
and pokes my heart. In your eyes
an urge and indulgence, a pair of chasing fireflies
shimmers forever in the past
Your clenched body, arms overlap
like vines round my waist (such warmth lasts a lifetime)
Magnetic sounds in your chest, a beehive
its faint feel of reproduction . . . Our only waltz:
my bare feet
step on your wide insteps
One two three, one two three
Eyes shut, the earth is immersed in your tall, straight branches
We're swirling, scattering leaves
Green, all green
Nothing else comes between us
Your whole body is a garden at last

月光曲

夜里，一些大胆的人在月光下睡觉
而我总是独自醒来
在这场梦幻里
长时间地睁着眼睛。床头，一只秃鹫在整理着羽毛

Moonlight Sonata

At night, a few bold ones sleep under the moonlight
I always wake up alone
in this dream
staring for a long time. At my bed, a vulture is arranging its feathers

在平原村

多么空寂啊
现在的村庄
没有少女的村庄

但是一种紫色的花儿在开放
在平一村
平二村
平三村
一树树的繁花淡淡地吐露芬芳
有些高过了屋瓦
有些，没进了绿色的水塘

我向一位倚着花树的老伯打听花名
他静静地看着我，笑而不语

In Pingyuan Village

How empty
a village today
one without maidens

But a purple flower is in full bloom—
in Pingyi Village
Ping'er Village
Pingsan Village
Tree by tree flowers flourish in soft fragrance
Some tower over roof tiles
Others, drowned in a green pond

To an old man against the flowering tree, I seek the flower name
Quietly he looks at me and answers with a smile

花间错

最喜食南瓜花
合着嫩南瓜和茎叶，揉碎，切细，生姜米爆炒
再加米汤煮透，嫩滑可口
金针花得焯过，滤水后才好用
草籽花清香馥郁
黄栀也吃得多，在水阁小镇，每年夏天
山脚的餐馆里都备着新鲜黄栀，一炒一大盘
木槿，可以干炸，也可以下汤
桂花我则搜集了当佐料，平时与糖一起贮存
生啖映山红如饮血
菊花与茉莉，都曾用于泡茶
至于玫瑰
我的一个朋友感慨道：你看那层叠的花瓣，那包含
不正是女子那象征么……
唉，我想我前世定是男儿身，以至今生混乱不堪
听了朋友的感慨，我竟也耳热心跳
止不住地浮想
细究起来，其实
不论是哪种花，不论怎样品尝
始终都散发着淡淡的清腥味儿，那清腥
几乎是对平淡生活的一种提醒

Flower Complex

I love eating pumpkin flowers most
tucked with tender pumpkin and stemmed leaves, minced, sliced, stir
      fried with ginger bits
then cooked with porridge, smooth and delicious
Blanch the orange daylilies. They cook better after being drained
Grass-seed flowers keep a strong fragrance
I also eat a lot of gardenias, every summer in small-town Shuige
Restaurants at the mountain's foot serve huge plates of fresh gardenias
Hibiscus can be deep-fried or used for making soups
I collect sweet olive as a condiment, usually stored with sugar
Eating raw azaleas is like drinking blood
Chrysanthemums and jasmines, used for brewing tea
As for roses
a friend lamented, *See these layered petals—do they not embody*
the symbol of a woman . . .
I must have been a man in my past life, utterly confused in this life
Upon my friend's words, my ears burned, my heart throbbed
and I couldn't help but imagine
Upon further thought, in fact
no matter what flowers, or how we savor them
they always exude a faint stench of freshness, a fresh stench
that almost reminds one of a plain life

酿造

采撷杨梅、葡萄、冰糖、糯米、红曲和水
我酿造了三种酒

漫长的黑暗中我等待着
血液中的三种品质：火热、坚硬和醇厚

Brew

Gathering waxberries, grapes, rock sugar, glutinous rice, red koji, and water
I brew three kinds of wine

In the sustained dark I wait
for three blood qualities: fiery, unyielding, richly mellow

雄黄

那日，青屋院中，一条虎斑游蛇
朝我竖起身躯
它昂首举颈，日头下
那鲜艳的红黑相间条纹
惊出我一身冷汗
于是回城后，穿街走巷
在西河沿的草药铺
寻得雄黄一包。店家嘱咐
"用酒浸泡后洒于院落四周，虫蛇不侵。"
此后忙乱，近两个月没去青屋
有时候在随身的手提袋里翻找东西，一下子
掏出了它——
一包雄黄
隔着透明塑料膜
这金灿灿、魅惑之物
每次都令我惊诧和恍惚
想那虎斑游蛇
只不过是与我一生中的某个时刻偶然相遇
而我，蝇营狗苟
活着仿佛只为抵抗这可见之物

Realgar

One day, in the courtyard in my green brick house, a tiger keelback
erected its body towards me
It reared up and raised its neck. Under the sun
stripes chequered with vivid red and black
scared me into a cold sweat
Back in the city, wandering through streets
I found a packet of realgar
in an herb shop along West River. The herbalist advised
Soak it in wine and sprinkle it around the courtyard; worms and
snakes will not invade
Almost two months now, I still haven't dropped by the green house
Rummaging through my carry bag now and then, I would fish it out
all at once—
a packet of realgar
through a transparent plastic membrane
A bewitching golden object:
it never fails to stun me into trance
I guess the tiger keelback
is but a chance encounter with some moment in my life
while I, in shameless pursuit of personal gain
live as though I could resist this visible thing

春水吟

"我们有多少余生可以共存?" 隔着几个省
你发来的询问依然湍急。眼前,是低吼的瓯江
一路翻山越岭而来
在此铺展,拐弯,打着旋,泛着恬淡的
要命的鱼腥味儿
我知道它隐秘的源头。在洞宫山西北,锅帽尖湿地
拔开枯黄的乱草
春天的新绿静静蛰伏
新绿之下,就是闪着亮光的细小水流
凛然、清冽,几近于无
流淌得悄无声息,却又义无反顾……
生命中,这些涌自心尖的战栗
我已学会暗暗汇集
在我今天的这个年龄,开始明白,一生
恰似这一去不复返的波涛
一江春水,形同一场辽阔的苦役
此刻,渡船在对岸抛锚了
师傅正忙着修理。埠头上
越来越多的人加入了静候的行列
一尾鱼突然跃出水面,有人惊呼出声
那银白色的肚腹
那一瞬即逝的闪电
唉,走神了,急湍湍的江水裹挟得我一阵晕眩

Hymn to the Spring Water

How many more years can we have together? From provinces away
you shoot me a snappy question. Before my eyes lies the growling River Ou
All the way, over hills and valleys
it sprawls through here, turns and swirls, suffused with a fatal
fishy stench, indifferent to fame or gain
I know its secret source: in southwestern Mount Donggong, a wetland
pushes aside messy dead weeds
A fresh spring green hibernates soundlessly
Beneath flows the glimmering river
Stern, cool, clear, almost a void
Quietly it runs, not turning back . . .
In life, I've learned to marshal shudders that surge
from the tip of my heart
At my age, I've begun to understand: a life
is like a wave, once gone forever lost
a spring river, like a vast toil
A ferryboat casts anchor at the opposite bank
Old boatmen mend their boats. On the pier
more join the quiet procession
A fish leaps out of the water, someone exclaims
A silver-white belly
An instant of lightning
I am distracted: the river wraps me into a daze

借着春风重新站好，远处江面上
成群的白鹭正盘旋飞舞
看哪，那俯冲下来的两只多么轻盈
雪白的翅膀斜刺进波涛，仿佛就要溯入这河流
就要明亮地消失
埠头的人群中，我也等待着

With spring wind I stand anew—far off
a congregation of egrets hovers in a waltz
Look, how graceful: two of them are diving down
White wings pierce the waves obliquely, as if to enter the river
                against its flow
and vanish in brightness
Among the crowd on the pier, I too wait

夜登山

我身上某个坚硬的地方
从不哭泣
那是夜色中山的一部分
是冷风中，迎面跑来的这个男子
两次呼吸之间，沉默的部分

越登高，山越晦暗
当我抬头，噢，一只庞大的黑猩猩

我吃了一枝掉落在地上
半干枯的拐枣
因为渴，我掬起一捧
流经山石和污物的溪水

当那股冰凉和浑浊从胸口坠下
我感觉到自己
咽下了黑夜的心

Mountain Night Climb

A hardened part of me
never weeps
A mountain limb in shades of night
A man runs into cold wind head-on
A silence between two breaths

The higher I reach, the darker it gets
When I lift my head, oh—a massive, black orangutan

I've eaten a branch of oriental raisins
half-shriveled aground
Thirsty, I cup with both hands
stream water flowing through rocks and muck

A chill and muddiness slump from my chest
I feel myself
swallow the heart of black night

如是我闻

夜晚。
可以是多汁的。
可以是黯哑的。
也可以是神秘的、莫测的。如同闹钟拥有的秘密心脏。

Thus Have I Heard

Night.
Can be juicy.
Can be pale.
Or mystical, unfathomable. Like the secret heart of an alarm clock.

入秋

月明时站在院子里发呆，凉风过处
已是日渐臃肿的妇人
电话里我说：这么快，就老了，淡了
甚至，不再对自己厌倦……多年来，是我内心的凶险
导致了世界的倾斜。看吧
秋天暗暗磨着的霜刀
亮了，它缺少滚烫的血———在我心中
也一直缺少一条恒河。因为这灵魂的罹难部分
所谓余生
也就是一种漫长的，不断康复的过程吧

Autumn Begins

At full moon, a cool breeze: I stare blankly in the courtyard
A woman bloats with time
How fast I age, I sigh over the phone. *Faded
and no longer weary of myself. . .* All these years, my inner perils
have forged a slanted world. Look
autumn sharpens its knife on the sly
Aglow, it lacks scalding blood—my heart
too lacks a Ganges, for the fatal part of this soul
the so-called twilight
is also a healing without end

寨头天浴

他袒露他的源头，在松阳寨头的天池里
或者，他褪下伦理
接近了美
风声多么高远，碧绿的天水汩汩而来，他纵身
自然的秩序
将生命一举到底
臀部浑圆、臂膀结实而紧凑
耸动如群山
朝日啊，将出未出，在水中荡漾

Bathing in the Open at Zhaitou

He bares his source in Lake Sky at Zhaitou
or takes his ethics off
to come close to beauty
How lofty the wind, jade green sky water gurgles on—he leaps
onto the natural order
and upholds life to its end
Perfect round buttocks, sturdy and compact arms
as stirring as mountains
O morning sun, soon to appear yet to appear, rippling on water

秋凉图

总是不够。日子
却又总是在拒绝中延续。我，有着人的混沌
和原始野兽的单纯

"你变了……"电话里你欲言又止
是么，我在秋风中竖起了衣领

愚钝如我，此生，没有旌旗，亦不设偶像
每每，只能以身体去认识世界
太多的事物，心灵无法转述。我习惯了
独自潮湿

我仅来自我变幻莫测的身体

Cool Autumn Painting

Never enough. Yet days
dilate in defiance. I carry human chaos
and the simplicity of wild beasts

You've changed . . . Over the phone my lover bites his tongue
Really? I turn up my collar in the autumn wind

Fool as I am, no banner or flags in this lifetime, no idols
My body is what acquaints me with the world
Too many things a soul can't paraphrase. Used
to getting wet on my own

I spring from my capricious body

战栗曲

被吞没，如雪片入海
我的惊呼，也不能使你停止

你这缄默的
海上的霸王，酝酿着浪花与浪花之间，肉体的喧响

你引领我消失
又在一片深深的湛蓝中，将我还原……你是个孩子
如此固执，在我复苏的土地上，寻找
生命的本初

我是多么地羞愧——神啊
一生，仿佛刚刚开始
微妙的幸福里，静静埋伏着不安

Song of Tremble

Devoured, like snow into sea
Even my alarmed cries can't stop you

You, this quiet
sea tyrant, brewing clamor of the flesh, between wave and wave

You lead me to disappearance
and restore me, again in this deep blue . . . You are a child
so stubborn, seeking in my revived land
the origin of life

I feel so ashamed—O Lord
a life seems to begin
Disquiet is ambushed in the subtle bliss

自我的洗礼

我总是失败，心灵却依然挣扎
我顾左右而言他
"为什么我不能延长在你的触摸之中？"
秋高气爽的日子里
我把血液中的蔚蓝还给天空
把影子
埋在了一棵橡树底下

Self-Baptism

At every turn I fail, but my heart still struggles
I beat around the bush
Why can't I unfurl in your touch?
In clear, crisp autumn
I return the sky the sky-blue in my blood
bury
my shadow under an oak

星夜的教育

我们，地球上的每一个丁
一定与天上的某一颗星辰相吻合吧
所以我们
不仅仅隔着高山、大海、林莽、沼泽或者戈壁
也不仅仅隔着年、月、日
我们之间应该是光年的距离
难以逾越和衡量
所以这些年，我一人
安之若素，一颗星，独自旋转
直到今年七月
在青屋的院子里
当我用五百二十五倍的天文望远镜搜寻夜空
才蓦然发现
大部分忽闪忽闪的星辰
其实都是双星，镜头里
两颗温润的小冰球，静静依偎
令我心跳如鼓
隔着亿万个光年
它们以无言的光辉
给予我初始的情感教育

A Starry Night Education

We—each a man on Earth
must be a good fit for a certain star in the sky
Thus are we set
apart by mountains, oceans, jungles, swamps, the Gobi
years, months, days
and the distance of light years
insurmountable, immeasurable
So all these years, alone
I have practiced equanimity, a star rotating on its own
until this July
in the courtyard inside my green house
when I comb the night sky with a telescope 525x
only to find
that most glittery stars are double
stars, each a pair of mild ice balls
in the lens, quietly nestled against each other
throbbing my heart like a drum
Set apart by billions of light years
bestowed on me with speechless splendor
the dawn of a sentimental education

PARTIAL SOLAR ECLIPSE

日偏食

她所经历的旅行
从来没有到达比自己更远的地方
也不能一劳永逸，"成为永久的大自然"
总得活着，总得去尝试
每一种新的错误
二十二日上午，丽水大地上，日偏食
世界的黄金被隐藏
她正骑车，从城北匆匆赶往城南
后面坐着需要托付的女儿
道路昏暗，凉气突袭
她骑得多么快啊
一阵越野的风
生活的路越狭窄，她飞行的欲望
越强烈

Partial Solar Eclipse

Her travels
can never transcend her selfhood
Nor can she, once and for all, *transform into the timeless nature*
One must live on and tackle
each new mistake
A partial solar eclipse in the morning on the twenty-second, upon Lishui
A cloak over the gold on earth
Riding an electric scooter, she rushes from the northern city to the south
Behind sits her daughter, in need of care
Gloomy path, a sudden chill
O how swiftly she rides
a cross-country wind
Roads narrow in life, her desire to soar
intensifies

枸杞

雾霾重重的古镇
小河边，谁家院。我们来
仿佛是为了与你相遇。我唤你
小心脏，小灯笼，小火焰，或者
琥珀耳垂，野蜂的蜜

雾霾重重，浮生若梦
传说中，如果要返回到人间
你就是那引路的小小灯盏

可我，多想携手走得更远一些
远到，前尘往事……任凭相依的剪影
在岁月的深处解体

Goji

Ancient town in smog and fog
Whose courtyard is it, by the river? We come
as if to meet you. I call you
little heart, little lantern, little flame, or
amber earlobe, wild bee honey

Smog and fog, life is but a dream
Legend has it, to return to the earthly world
you would be the little lamp leading the way

But how I wish to go farther, hand in hand
until the sentient past . . . no matter how silhouettes side by side
dissolve deep in years

初遇

爸妈地间，哥哥在上学
我一个人
去了后院。这是六月，大洋湖宽广明亮
粼粼的波光，荡向远方
在我短缺的童年
水，是我和伙伴们唯一的快乐
——我已偷偷学会了游泳
笨拙的狗刨式。这是童年，六月的一天
第一次，我一人
独自步入水中
绿色的湖水，若有若无，托着我的头颅
像颗孤单的水葫芦
我安静地漂浮着，表面明亮、温暖
愈往下，愈冰冷，愈幽深
凉意沿着脊椎骨，漫上我的胸口
有如命运给予的补偿，渐渐地
我开始步入了
一个从未体验的世界
涌动着莫名的兴奋和隐隐的恐惧，在那
看不见的深处
暗流阵阵，无穷的未知潜伏着
鱼和小虾围拢米，一下一下
轻啄着我的胳膊、胸脯和双腿

First Encounter

Our parents were working in the fields, my brother at school
On my own
I went out to the backyard. It was June: a wide bright Lake Dayang
sparkling waves, washing faraway
In my meager childhood
water was the only joy for my pals and me
—secretly I had learned to swim
the clumsy dog paddle. This was my childhood, a day in June
For the first time, I stepped
alone into water
Green lakewater in a haze, cupping my skull
like a lonely water hyacinth
I floated quietly, luminous and warm
Lowering further, icier, the tranquil deep
A chill down the vertebra seeped into my chest
like a compensation from fate, gradually
I stepped
into an alien world
billowing with thrill beyond words, faint fear, in that
unseen depth
undercurrents an infinite unknown
Fish and shrimp crowded around, bit by bit
pecking at my arm, chest, and legs

我不知道，贴着我腰际凉凉滑过的
到底是水蛇还是鳗
不远处，分开的大钳锯后面
蟹正转动着电光般犀利的凸眼
螺丝从脚趾缝里挤出来
又随着淤泥淌走。那脚底的蚌
它粗糙、沉默的石头身体，会突然向我
张开它紧闭的黑暗吗？

I couldn't tell if a water snake or an eel
glided coolly past my waist
Close at hand, behind its open forceps
a crab was rotating its electric convex eyes
Screws squeezed through from between my toes
and oozed away with the silt. Would the mussel
under the sole—its coarse, silent stone-body—suddenly open
its sealed darkness to me?

铁皮桶

随着麻绳"嘣"的一声断裂，盛满水的
铁皮捅，消失在幽深的井中

我绕着井沿转悠，不敢回家
哥哥闻讯赶来，一帮小后生，激烈地讨论

"我下去吧！"哥哥最后做出了决定
他脱下外衣，开始为下井做着准备

围观者越来越多，人们等待着
有人送来一杯烧酒，一个生鸡蛋

烧酒一仰脖就喝光了，那个用锥子
戳了个小洞的生鸡蛋，哥哥则吸了好长时间

他把看起来似乎是完好的空鸡蛋放到我手上
光着膀子，最后看我一眼，我打了一个冷战

——啊请原谅，我的记忆出现了中断
三十年前，一只铁皮桶，坠入深深的井中

A Metal Pail

With a "snap" the hemp rope severed, a metal pail
of water vanished into the unruffled well

Afraid of going home without it, I loitered
Brother rushed here upon hearing the news. A band of youths
in heated discussion

I'll go down! At last, Brother made up his mind
took off his coat, and started to ready himself for the well

A crowd gathered, we waited
Someone offered a cup of sorghum wine, a raw egg

In a gulp, he emptied the cup. A hole was poked
in the egg with an awl. He sucked at it for a long time

and placed the perfect-looking egg on my hand
Shoulders naked, he took a last glance at me as I shuddered

—O please forgive me, a blackout in my memory
Thirty years ago, a metal pail fell into a deep well

哥哥是否最终将它捞起，还是多年来
它一直潜在那底下，作为我人生的暗物质？

画面已然模糊不清。但我记得那个貌似完好的鸡蛋
那个战栗；记得井沿边，那种幽深、虚空的冷

Did Brother scoop it out, or is it still lurking deep
down, as the dark matter of my life?

The scene is now a blur. Yet I recall the perfect-looking egg
the shudder; I recall, by the well, the unruffled depth, a hollow cold

枯水期

每年到了盛夏
槐湖就会干涸上几天，露出河床来
鱼都到哪儿去了呢？我把手伸进洞穴，摸到了
一条尾巴：光滑、扁平、躁动……用力一抓
那只手，却被狠狠地
咬了一口，尖锐且刺痛，从那
深深的，看不见的地方

Dry Season

At high summer
Lake Huai runs dry a few days, the bed revealed
Where are the fish? I stretch my hand into the grotto, touch
a tail: sleek, flat, fidgety . . . a violent seizure
My hand suffers
a harsh bite, sharp and prickly, from that
deep, invisible site

小镇的回忆

群山之中的南方小镇
四季分明，河水徜徉
道路两旁耸立着高大、笔直的水杉
小镇的水阁中学里，我是一名乡村女教师
享有一间废弃的教室
里面一床、一桌、一椅
授课之余，得以一人独处
整整十年，我过着一种单纯的生活
"那为什么还要改行呢？"每每人们这样问及
我总是暗自羞愧，嗫嚅着
不知如何作答
实际上，我早已习惯了漫长的孤独
不能忍受的，只是日复一日
面对一双双天真的、懵懂的眼睛。离开小镇越远
我越清楚，关于我
真正的启蒙，均非来自教育

Memories of a Small Town

A small town among mountains in the south
Four distinct seasons, a river loiters free
Dawn redwoods line each path, towering on both sides
In this small town, I teach at Shuige Junior High
A discarded classroom
A bed, a table, a chair
After my classes, I'm on my own
Ten whole years, I lead a simple life
So why change vocation? When people ask
I blush in shame and stammer
not knowing what to say
Truth is, I've grown used to solitude
What I can't bear is the day-in-day-out
facing pair after pair of clueless eyes. The farther I live
the clearer I know, when it comes to me
real learning does not begin at school

后园

我好久，没有去过后园
那潮湿小径，背对着我的
秘密生长，仿佛
时光之外
梧桐树，萧萧落下，满地的金黄
我抬头看见，树桠间的黄昏，以及黄昏里
往返盘旋的鸽群，院子上空，或内心
那些深深浅浅的划痕……
我的脚在碎瓦上，下沉，不由自主，跌进
身体的裂缝。我想起
多少个夜里我曾暗自抚摸，那么多
无法掩埋的
黑色蚂蚁，涌出了，后园
蓬松的洞穴

Backyard

For a long time, I have not stepped into the backyard
A small damp path facing my back
grows in secret, as if
beyond time
wutong leaves rustle and fall, a golden floor
I raise my head, watch the dusk through forking branches; within it
I see pigeons hover to and fro, or multiple
scratches on my heart . . .
On shattered tiles, my feet sink and I fall
into my body cracks. I recall
the nights when I stroked my body and mind in darkness, so many
black ants
that couldn't be buried, outpouring in the backyard
from a fluffy cave

黎明前夕

父亲总是在最前面
握着锄头轻轻挥舞，嚓、嚓、嚓
鲜嫩的春笋应声倒下

母亲紧随其后，一根根捡起

竹叶和泥巴沾到了装笋的麻袋上
又湿漉漉地掉下

如果，我的哥哥还在
他会朝我竖起食指："嘘——"

曙光到来之前
春笋破土拔节的声音
在幽暗潮湿的竹园子里，在这里，那里——

The Eve of Dawn

Always in the lead
Father wields a hoe and swings it gently, *Cha, cha, cha*
Fresh bamboo shoots fall in response

Close behind, Mother picks them up one by one

Bamboo leaves and mud stick to the sack
before sliding off soggily

Were Brother still alive
he would, an index finger over his lips, say *Shhh*—

Before dawn
voices of shoots in their joint stage
emerge from the dim bamboo garden: here, there—

再一次的古镇

你说要带我一起飞
使得我成了一个心事过重的人

今晚，再次夜宿古镇
我选择在远一些的地方
遥看我们曾经停留过的青石埠头

还有那渡口客栈
带斜坡的阁楼间。木地板洁净，我们双双
赤着脚

我已不年轻，但依然会胆怯
依然需要你的鼓励——明月在窗
在那一个瞬间里，我存活

你是否记得这银镜似的江面呢
江两岸，深黛色的林子和山峦绵延无边

今夜空空的埠头，下弦月
照耀着亘古的空寂。没来由的，我颤抖
却不是来自你的触摸

Ancient Town Again

Your words, *Let me take you on my wings*
weigh on my mind

Again, we spend a night in an ancient town
I choose to gaze from far
at a limestone pier where we once lingered

and the ferry inn
with a gable roofed attic. Clean wooden floor, our feet
naked

No longer young, but still timid
I need your encouragement—bright moon at the window
I survive in such fugitive instant

Do you recall our silvery river
On its banks, dark turquoise groves, an infinite mountain range

Tonight an empty pier, the half moon
illumines an undying emptiness. For no reason, I tremble
but not for your touch

有些话，你说了，可能就忘了
更不会懂得
你对我的生活做了什么

再一次，一个人的古镇
我来，是为了将恐惧提前消耗

Words you've said, now forgotten
let alone know
what you've done to my life

Again, ancient town, all to myself
I come to spend fear in advance

水边

大雁低低地
擦过我们的头顶。黄昏也低低地
推过来白色的波涛
"变是唯一的不变"。在水边
除却了身上，所有的衣物
我们是闪亮的白银，即将升起的月光，星辰
是水，回到了水

By the Water

Low wild geese
brush over our heads. Low dusk
coaxes white waves
Change is the only constant. By the water
bodies stripped bare
we shimmer white silver, rising moonlight, stars
as water, back to water

草事

那年经过草塔
我指着路边的地名感慨：我喜欢
和草有关的事物
你正开车，手把方向盘，快速地侧过脸
看了一下

嗯，快速地，然后继续行驶。经过草塔
经过那草一样的我

其实我喜欢的还有很多：
草书、萱草、草鱼、《枕草子》、草庵、《徒然草》……
我连着用了几年的佰草集
在机场候机，因为一个店铺叫食草堂
不由自主，我转进去好几次

而每次去山里的青屋
门前和院落里，迎接我的
尽是一人多高的野草

"独怜幽草涧边生"啊
说到底，这些，毕竟是我个人的事

Grass-things

One year, passing Grass Tower
I pointed at the place name and sighed, *I love
anything about grass*
You were driving, hands on the wheel, before turning your face
for a quick glance

Yes, quick, then on with the road. Past Grass Tower
and the grassy me

I too enjoy
cursive, tiger lily, grass carp, *The Pillow Book*, a grass hut, *Essays in Idleness* . . .
and a few years of "Herborist" skin products
Once, at an airport, I couldn't help but frequent
the shop Herbal Heaven

Whenever I drop by my mountain green house
wild grass taller than a man
greets me at the door, in the courtyard

Alone, I savor wildflowers tucked in along the creek
Bottom line: these are *my favorite things*

不如看荒木经惟谈写真术，却听他笑道：
哎呀！怎么可以聊这么深入的问题呢！
我只想"在浅草的午后，与你一起缠绵"。
——呵呵，果然是大师

How about studying portraiture with Nobuyoshi Araki? Araki laughs,
My! How can we chat about such profound truth!
All I want is "an erotic afternoon with you in Asakusa."
—a Maestro indeed

夜读莫拉小说

"干脆把这些都忘掉吧。"他蜷在围椅里
身子往后靠了靠，
"就像我忘了走，把自己忘在这里
忘在这间房子里一样。"
那双搭在椅子上的手，开始呈现出
木质的颜色和纹理……我揉了揉眼睛
哦，夜深了
"其实很多人，就是这样
留在生活里的。"他继续说。

Reading a Mora Novel at Night

Just forget it. He curls up in an armchair
and leans his body backward,
Like me when I forget to leave, forgetting myself here
in this room.
Hands on the chair start to display
a wooden color and texture. I rub my eyes
O, deep night
To this end, he continues,
most of us are stuck in life.

等待或其它

帷幕落下了。留在空荡的剧场内
我等待着，时光背后
未知的另一场。我相信自己，对于世界
最初的感觉。比如相信一本书，将不停地翻开
难以确定的下一页。一本
《沙之书》，藏在阿根廷图书馆尘封的架子上
没有开头和结尾，其间
我们各自隐藏——作为细节和插图，是无限，也是短暂

Waiting or Et Cetera

Curtains down. Alone in the empty theater
I wait, behind time
another unknown scene. I believe in my first impression
of the world. When I believe in a book, I would keep flipping
to the next nonspecific page. A copy
of *The Book of Sand*, tucked away on a dusty shelf in the National
       Library of Argentina
Without a beginning and an end, in the thick
of the story we each hide—as detail and illustration, infinite yet transient

寅夜书房

我一直坐到寅时，但并未就此
增添了多少知识

我在读过的书页中，留下众多的折痕，可我
是健忘的。况且时光飞逝
有什么，正在沙沙地消失……

"不会有来生，不会有……"不止一次，我就这样
盯着你的眼睛。而此刻，你又在哪里？
"神是那潮汐涨落的大海，涌动不息。"
我一个人背诵，我一个人

和案头上，那盆多年不开花的君子兰一起
渴望生活，而非等待奇迹

In the Study Late at Night

I stay up into the small hours, but fail
to understand the words

I make fold marks, but they can't keep things from slipping
my mind. Time evaporates
Something shuffles, vanishes . . .

No, there won't be a next life . . . More than once, I stare
into your eyes. Where are you?
God is the sea, the billows, the ebb and flow
I recite, alone

at the desk, a pot of clivia years from flowering
yearning for life, but not waiting for a miracle

相遇

街头，拐角处，你叫着
惊异地拉住我"这么多年，你去了哪儿？"
我不知该如何描述——

或许一直以来，我都不在，我的生活里
或许，我打开了每天的嘴和眼睛
活着，十年如一日……
你开始沉浸到自己，纷繁的过去
那些爱情、车马、异地
那些狂欢和失去

你说"心都碎了。"我默默地低头，看地
在我们的脚边，时间多么迅速
蜂拥的黑蚁，悄无声息，围拢
一只死去的小虫

Encounter

On a street corner, you stop me
in surprise, *Where've you been all these years?*
I don't know where to begin—

Who knows if I've never been around
Day after day, my mouth and eyes open:
a monotonous life . . .
You start to indulge in your byzantine pasts
those romances, cars and horses, exotic lands
those wild joys and losses

But you confess, *My heart is broken.* Quietly I bow my head
and look down at our feet—how time flies
Black ants flock around
a dead bug

知青回城

在板车和垃圾池之间
我那矮小的母亲，显得多么有力
她挥舞着铁锹
奋力地铲着，铲着，仿佛在将一生
重新搬运

垃圾清运工——这是回城后
知青母亲的第一份工作
"如果能转正就好了……"
她干得满天大汗，毫不嫌弃

小区里总是有人走过
我站得尽可能的远
尽可能的。隔着
整整一个时代（那是否
我幼年的羞耻心？）

板车满了。一前一后
母亲与我，倾尽全身
推拉着笨重的板车出城

卸下，扒拉干净，插回屉板
叉着腰小憩——我的母亲
有生之年，你始终心有不甘
喘着粗气，翘望着将你放逐的都市

A Sent-Down Youth Is Back in Town

Between the handcart and the leachate
my petite mother looked so strong
She brandished her spade
With every effort she shoveled on and on, as if transporting
a lifetime anew

Dustwoman—this was Mother's first job
as a sent-down youth back in town
A permanent status, how wonderful life would be . . .
Not minding the labor, the sweat

Whenever someone passed by
I would stand as far as I could
The farthest possible: an era
apart (was that
my childhood shame?)

The handcart was full. Back and front
we pushed and pulled its weight
out of town

Unloaded, shoved, cleaned, the handcart adjusted
Hands on her waist for a rest—O Mother
you panted and looked up at the city that banished you
All your life, you felt unreconciled

你的背后，是我
母亲。你把我搁置在
这个世界的边缘
在城乡结合地带
在一堆垃圾刚刚倾倒出的新鲜腐味里
让我看清了
合乎自己尺寸的命运——
草籽花无边无际
机耕路旁，青蒿疯长，豆荚
撑出嘎嘎的破裂声

Mother, I was right behind
you. You had shelved me away
to the edge of the world
where the country and the city merged
in the fresh foul stench of a dumped rubbish pile
where I saw
a destiny, tailor-made—
boundless grass-seed flowers
by a tractor path, an overgrowth of sweet wormwood, bean pods
holding out pieces of screaky cries

停留

那年我七岁。出了后院，午后的槐湖
是一面巨大的明镜

我在蔚蓝的湖边洗手帕，白色
如同水波里荡漾开去的云朵
突然，手帕下沉了，一伸手，整个人
落进了水中……太深了，我的双脚
够不着水底，也没有爬上岸的力气

没有呼救声。只是紧紧地
抓住了埠头上的青石板——真安静哪
四周无人，一片沉寂。头顶上
天蓝蓝的，白云慢吞吞的
比倒映在湖水里的，更高些、更远些。没有呼救声

在众多的告诫中，我一直害怕
斥责，一直停留在
广大的世界和微小的心灵之间
保持着沉默

Pause

That year I turned seven. Outside the backyard one afternoon, Lake Huai
glared like a huge mirror

By the azure lake I washed a handkerchief, its whiteness
like water clouds undulating out
The handkerchief sank. I stretched my hand, fell
headlong into the water . . . My legs
couldn't touch the bed. Too weak to climb

ashore, I grabbed
onto the pier's green slabstone—not a soul
stood, dead stillness. Overhead
the sky was clear, clouds sluggish
farther, taller than reflections in the lake. I didn't yell for help

Warned beforehand, I feared
reproach. Between
the august world and my teeny soul, I paused
to maintain silence at all costs

在我母亲家的庭院

母亲和女儿上楼去了
浇灌过的园子，散发着泥土的潮腥。坐在草坪上
不愿起身，我仿佛
一个远去之物

只有泰迪犬可可，安静地靠着我
我本该上楼去
握住她的手，轻声劝说——
我的母亲，中国最早的知青，发育出了晚年
一颗暴怒的心

植物在渴饮
一种低低的呻吟
啊母亲，为何你不能时时温存
像对待你栽下的，这满园的无名花草呢？

……父亲还在出走中
那不眠之夜，多么刻骨……

我本该起身但我坐着没动
一切皆有源头
来自那特殊的时代
来自那没有温度的结合，母亲，我的寒冷
是否诞生于你？

In Mother's Courtyard

Mother has gone upstairs with my daughter
Her just-watered garden reeks of fish and mud. Sitting on the lawn
reluctant to get up, I feel
remote—

Coco the poodle leans calmly against me
I ought to have gone upstairs
hold her hand, coax softly,
Dear Mother, a pioneer sent-down youth, a heart of wrath
in twilight years

Thirsty plants drink
a low moaning
O Mother, why can't you be gentle all the time
like treating your garden of nameless flowers and grass?

. . . An insomniac night:
Father ran away from home—a memory so deep-rooted . . .

I sit still even though I shouldn't
Everything happens for a reason
An uncommon era
an icy union: Mother, did I inherit
your coldness?

不觉间双眼湿热、模糊。你刚刚
带着我女儿浇花的身影，如同和煦的夕阳
还在草木间晃动
而我，只是看着，听着，仿佛一个远去之物

可可依然安静，前些时
它滚滚的卷毛被全部剃尽，这会儿，正有些丑陋地
迎接它的成年

My eyes turn moist, hot, and blurry. Your silhouette
as you water the flowers with your granddaughter, sways like a sunset
among the greenery
Feeling remote, I watch and listen

Coco stays calm and hushed
Shaved to ugly, it now welcomes
its coming-of-age

果园

椪柑挂果后，父亲抱着被子
住到了果园的窝棚里。他深谙
耕耘和收获之间的关系

我去了哪里？当我回顾
孩提时的果园，只有父亲不成调的
调子，哼唱在林子各处

是啊，那时起，我就常常消失
跟随一阵莫名的风
一行雉鸡的爪痕
一个枝桠上的巢穴
一簇新鲜的，刚刚打出的泥洞

没有任何扶助
也没有信仰的眷顾
一个在山林间野大的孩子，胡乱地
走到今天，灵魂里
有着太多的缺页

我已无法找到身上的某些部分
果园的泥土里
埋藏着幼虫的一生。当我回顾

Orchard

Once the ponkans bore fruit, Father took a quilt
to stay in the shack, mindful
of ushering *labor* to *harvest*

Where was I? As I recall
the childhood orchard, only Father hummed
tunelessly through the grove

Yes, from then on I had disappeared
along with a gust of ineffable wind
a trace of pheasant claw
a nest on twigs
a cluster of mud holes freshly dug

Without any help
or care for faith
a wild child in the mountain woods has muddled
through her way till now, her soul
missing too many pages

No longer can I recover parts of my body
Buried in the mud
in the orchard is a larva's lifetime. As I recall

一个小时，或更久
一只童年的蛹
从那盔甲中慢慢地爬出，解脱，倒挂
亮开纤薄双翅

for an hour or perhaps longer
a childhood pupa
climbs out of its armor, free, hanging upside down
its thin wings in a bright spread

一个例行散步者的碎语

为了不至于重复
每天的散步
我选择不同的时辰和方向出行
进入不同的街区
汇入不同的生命的河流

路过一个个不同的你
我捕捉那不可重复的音容笑貌，吸纳着
每一丝独特的人间气息
我明白时间有限
我和你，也许永不重逢
只为了我心中
对这世界奔腾的爱意
只为了使这短促的一生得以稍稍延长

有时夜深人静
我偶然停留，被映在沿街橱窗里的自己惊醒
独自呆愣半晌

有时，斜阳尚好
沿着街道向阳的这边一直走远
回来时经过它背阴的对面
一路上，踩着发黑的

Fragments of a Seasoned Stroller's Soliloquy

To thwart repetition
in my daily strolls
I choose a different time and direction
enter different streets
into different rivers of life

Because of my love for this world
and a desire
to outlast this lifetime
I pass by each and every different *you*
catch each voice and expression, absorb
each strand of mortal breath
I accept the limits of time
and know that I may never meet you again

Late and all quiet
I linger around, roused by my reflection in the shop window
alone and stunned

Now and then, a fair setting sun
I keep walking far on the sun-doused side of the street
and in the opposite shade on my way back
All along, I trample

未曾融化的积雪
如同踩着我体内固执和残缺的部分
在北京早春
生冷的夜风里，我双手捂着耳朵
几乎要落下泪水

the blackened snow
as if trampling a stubborn, deformed part in my body
In the early spring of Beijing
against a cold, raw night wind, I cover my ears with both hands
on the verge of tears

夜行列车上的心碎者

列车过金华，漫长的中转
硬卧车厢。折叠小凳。她缩紧身子
贴着窗玻璃，不出声，尽量与黑夜
保持着一致

山峦黝黝，远灯如豆
连绵相似的风景，此处，亦是他处
然而……金华……一个尘封的瞬间突然
浮现，猛地击中了她

二十多年前，哥哥送她
赶赴金华考学。贫寒兄妹，搭上了
一辆过路的货车
到了金华郊外，他们被卸下
哥哥背着她的绘画工具，牵着她的手
徒步至市区
详细叮嘱后，告别返家

而她，一头扎进了
属于她自身的命运漩涡里，从未回头
和停驻，也从未细想：
从金华到丽水，一百多公里，她那
无以生计的哥哥
是如何返的家？

A Broken Heart Takes the Night Train

The train passes through Jinhua for a layover
A hard sleeper carriage. Stool folded. She huddles her body up
presses against the window, staying in harmony
with the night

A range of black mountains and beanlike lamps
An infinite landscape where here is elsewhere
yet . . . Jinhua . . . out of the blue, a dust-
sealed instant strikes

Twenty years ago, Brother sent her off
for her entrance exams in Jinhua. Penniless, they caught
a random cargo truck
and alighted in the suburbs
Brother carried her drawing tools, took her hand
and walked to town
After rounds of instructions, he bid her farewell and set for home

But she plunged headlong
into her destiny—a whirlpool—never turned back
or stopped to reflect:
from Jinhua to Lishui, over a hundred kilometers
how did her unemployed brother
find his way home?

啊不，她不明白自己怎能如此轻佻——
……惊悸突袭，她蓦地明白
原来哥哥，并非罹难于
一场车祸，她早已失去了他
在多年前
在此地，那个她不曾回头的
告别的瞬间……哐当声中，列车重又启动
却似乎掉了个头
开往来时的方向。泪水中她愕然
随即又闭眼，更紧地贴着窗户，一个
心碎者管不了一列夜行的火车
一段不堪的人生，一个追问

No, she can't understand how frivolous she was—
... a spasm of terror and realization:
Brother died not
from a car accident; she had long lost him
years back
here, in that moment of farewell
when she did not once turn back ... In a rattle, the train picks up
yet seems to turn around
and head backward. Stunned in tears
eyes shut, she presses closer against the window. A
heartbroken soul can't control a night train
a deplorable life, such scrutiny

IN SEARCH OF PORCELAIN

我的山国

有一年春天，我在乡下的青屋里
平息了身体的波浪

也曾夜观星象。在院中，用高倍望远镜
搜寻着大大小小的月坑
一座座亘古的环形山，对应着浙西南
我蛰居的谷地
没有欢乐，没有悲伤

常去的是附近的峡谷
坐在溪石上，四野寂寂，青峰朗朗
听周遭草木隐忍地拔节而不惊

直到，一天晌午，几声短促的呼哨后
一只红嘴蓝雀
出现在视野上方，它那长长的
凤尾似的白羽，优雅从容，静止在山谷
瓦蓝的空中……哦这孤独的翔翔
这山国岁月，秘密的赐予——我的心

碎了。万物在春天，皆有分裂的痛
而我，有了深处的动静

My Mountain Country

One spring, in my country green house
I appeased my body waves

and observed stars at night. In the courtyard, I searched for lunar craters
big and small with a high-power telescope
One by one, timeless impact craters mirrored Southwest Zhejiang
No joy, no sorrow
in the valley where I lived secluded

I hung around the canyon nearby
Quiet all around, summits green and bright, I sat on a stream rock
listened to grass and trees endure the jointing stage in silence and
            indifference

until one noon, after some urgent whistles
a red-billed blue magpie
appeared atop the horizon, its long
white feather like a phoenix tail, elegant and calm, resting at the valley
in an azure sky . . . O this solitary soar
these mountain country years, the secret bestowal—my heart

broke. In spring, all things on earth share the pain of fission
and I found movement deep down

七月漫游

七月，回到南方的杉树林
遇见了寒鸦
和草尖上的一滴血。什么东西走过去了
梅雨期，轻描淡写，留不住
一个身体的温度……我在深夜的井边哭泣
听见了山后
大雁的声音。我经过的
都是些短暂的
永恒？我重又抵达这个地点，却已不再是
那个时间……你还好吗
你们还好吗……但愿
群山深处
我的亲人和朋友呵
在我居无定所的形骸里，继续生长
在万物中安然无恙——

Wandering in July

July, back to fir woods in the south
crossing paths with a jackdaw
and a drop of blood on grass tip. Whatever in passing—
plum rain season, an understatement—can't restrain
a body's temperature . . . I weep by the well late at night
listen to voices
of wild geese behind the mountain. Is what I pass by
some transient
eternity? I arrive again at this place, but am no longer
of that time . . . How've you been
How've you all been . . . May
my kin and friends
deep in the mountains
in my rootless body, continue to grow
safe and sound in the universe—

莲花峰日记

我把自己，安顿在了
布满丛林的莲花峰上。一段坡路
一扇风雨中的，小小院门

打雷的夜晚我也出去了，一趟趟
我往房间里添置着家电、日用品、书籍、食物
添置着色彩、声音和气味

在后山，我还掘到了不知名的兰草
湿漉漉地回来，喘着气
——摆放好我的生活……似乎

我不再缺什么了，我还缺什么呢
风正从坡上灌进屋子，站在房中央
忍不住，哭了。九月五日

Lotus Summit Diary

I've found a place for myself
in the woody Lotus Summit. A stretch of hill road
a tiny gate in wind and rain

On stormy nights I too go out, round after round
To my room I add appliances, everyday essentials, books, food
add colors, voices, and scents

In the back hill, I've even picked nameless bonesets
Back in wetness, I pant
and arrange my life piece by piece . . . I no longer

seem to lack anything, what do I still lack
Wind pours in from the slope. Standing in the center of the room
I can't help but cry. September 5

寻瓷记

在抚摩和亲近你之前
我先亲近了翡翠的冷辉、溪水
溪水边的光滑石子、一滴
清脆响亮的鸟鸣

你并不停留在自身
"雨过天青云破处"
或者对称，或者左右均衡
你的每一次移动，那完美弧度
都引诱着我
再次的出发和跟随

因为你，我爱上了去探寻
事物隐秘的核心、你躯体的曼妙中轴
爱上了泥和水的浑然交媾
闭上眼，贴近，细细聆听
你平静的深渊里
烈焰，满怀失身的激情

In Search of Porcelain

Before fondling you, I grew
intimate with the cold jade glow and the stream
Slick pebbles by the water, a drip
of crisp, sonorous bird call

You never confine yourself to what you are
After rain, comes a clear sky
In symmetry or balance, right and left
your every move, its perfect radian
lures me
to start afresh and follow along

Because of you, I'm in love with a quest
for the hidden core of things, a lithe axial lobe in your body
I'm in love with mud and water, the perfect copulation
Eyes shut, I lean close to listen
in your calm abyss
to roaring flames, a chestful of passion from lost virginity

风继续吹

从群峰中涌出
越澹真岛、过长桥、临湖听水
我想我和风
已互为一体。吴山脚下
叫上一份米酒
这粗陶的器皿，让人喜欢
给自己斟满，当空举起：
"晚来天欲雪，能饮一杯无？"
你是否听见，喉头
滚动一声？你野蛮起来像个土匪
当我喊出"疼"，冷淡已然出现
并非因为此刻，并非因为你
这悲哀早已成型……风继续吹着
嗨，等我喝完这杯。放弃
意味着更大的勇气——
如我今日
不画画，不写诗，不怨恨，也不爱恋
如果我安静下来
如果你安静下来
风会吹送，我们相遇的瞬间
我停留在那里，很轻
失去了任何形式

Wind Goes On

Gushing from summits
past Danzhen Island and Long Bridge, listening to the lake
I must have blended
with the wind. At the foot of Mount Wu
I order rice wine for one
What a charming earthernware vessel
I fill it to its brim and hold it up high, *You've come late. Heaven's*
verging on snow. You'll stay and share a cup or two, won't you?
Can you hear the tumble
in your throat? Like a bandit, how barbaric you are
When I yell out *pain*, apathy has surfaced
Grief has found its figure
not because of you or now . . . Wind goes on
Wait for me to finish this cup of wine. To relinquish
stands for more courage—
like me now
who neither paints, writes, resents, nor falls in love
If I quiet down
If you quiet down
wind will unite us in a second
I'll linger, very lightly
any form or shape lost

满月

九曜山、莲花峰、玉皇山、南屏山
无论走到哪
不经意地抬头，一轮银盘
都静静地挂在坡顶上。广阔、充盈，似乎
一动未动……而群山之中
我则夜夜逡巡
朗朗明月之下，唯有
仰望、噤声
这颗喑哑的心啊，它只是
一本书中，两个段落间的空白
抑或，一片混沌——有什么
还远远地，没有出生

Full Moon

Mount Jiuyao, Lotus Summit, Mount Yuhuang, Mount Nanping
No matter where I go
I raise my head, the moon a galactic disc
hangs over the slope crest. Vast, plentiful, as if
immobile . . . Yet among mountains
I prowl each night
under the bright moon, only
to look up, speechless
O this mute heart, just
an empty space between two paragraphs
or chaos—what else
stays unborn, far and away

出门

打开小屋时，阳光已经
照耀莲花峰多日了。土坡泛着白
何首乌爬得到处都是
斑驳的阴影，和潮湿……这一刻
阳光也照着我，照着这另外的
一小块潮湿

Going Out

When I open the hut, sunlight has
been shining on Lotus Summit for days. Slopes are suffused with white
Chinese knotweeds climb everywhere
Mottled shadows and moisture . . . At this instant
sunlight too shines on me, this other
patch of moisture

上山

草丛里窸窣作响。小松鼠
拖着蓬松的大尾巴，在枝桠间
倏忽一闪。空山。鸟语。频频振羽之声
多么细小、无处不在的……荡漾
"心灵是个孤独的猎人。"我喜欢
这样细细地造访：
枯草、呼吸、洞穴、尚有体温的毛羽
我喜欢逐一确认，这世间万物，隐秘
而丰厚的心灵。它们
不比一道光线明亮
却比人心，久远得多了

回来的路上，一颗小榛子从头顶"啪"地落下
停在了我的脚边
我把它紧紧地攥在手心里
直到它，整个地发热。我知道，这是大山
给予我的，温润的馈赠

Up the Mountain

Grass rustles. A squirrel
hauls a fluffy tail, an instantaneous flash
among twigs and branches. Empty mountain. Birds sing. Flapping
       feathers
so minute, yet ubiquitous . . . in ripples
The heart is a lonely hunter. I relish
such a fine visit:
withered grass, breath, grotto, feathers still with body heat
I like to confirm lavish spirits, one by one
cloaked in this universe. Each
no brighter than a ray of light
but more ancient than mortal hearts

On the way back, a hazel falls from above, lands with a "thud"
by my feet
I hold it tightly in my palm
until it glows with heat. This is the mountain's
warm, humid gift

白云山记

山涧断流了
袒露着白花花的溪石
可还是有很多人把自己散落在这里
沿着溪涧慢慢往上
可以看到一些人世间的浮云
停留在竹林丛中
或者高低错落的巨石边上
一对年轻的云朵正紧紧地依偎
用赤足搅动着积存的水洼。山风习习
我的脚下有松针，过于绵软
心脏咚咚跳着
我不知该如何行走
才能在这山中，将自己安放

Chronicle of Mount White Cloud

A mountain stream broke
its shiny white rocks exposed
yet people scatter themselves here
Slowly up the stream
clouds drift from the mortal world
pausing among bamboo groves
or on boulders strewn at random
Two young clouds leaning close
stir a puddle with naked toes. A mountain breeze
Pine needles feel too soft under my feet
My heart throbs
I don't know how to walk
to place myself safely in this mountain

在黑夜里经过万家灯火

车灯亮着，前面坡地上，黑夜留出了
一小块的空白……在森林公园，一切
都静下来了，夜鸟、树桠间的风、
以及山脚下
一个城池的灯火——
我曾置身其间啊，多少个夜晚，多少年
没有呼应地微弱与单薄

都静下来了，而我无端啜泣
站在寂静的白云山顶
回望阑珊处，这些辉煌或卑微的闪烁
仿佛灵魂，今晚
我一一经过，一一经过

Passing by Thousands of City Lights in Black Night

Headlights on: black night lays aside a void
on the front slope . . . In the forest park, all
quiet: night birds, wind between tree forks
a city of lights
at the mountain's foot—
O how I was once soaked in it, nights and years
passive and frail

All quiet, for no reason I sob
atop Mount White Cloud
Looking back at dim lights—bright or humble
soul-sparks—tonight
I'll pass by them, one by one by one

山上的小屋

是风，在拍打着杉树皮的屋顶
我总是埋着头。屋子外面，许多草叶
越过了栅栏
在山中奔跑。风声里，我总是
忘记了时间
或者季节。那握住
又松开的掌心，纵横交错的
命运——我记得，我有过五月
和蓝色星空下作出的诺言
我曾经归来……一次又一次
在后院
埋下了种子、错失和爱

A Mountain Hut

Wind whacks the fir-bark roof
I bow my head low. Outside my house, grass and leaves
arch over fences
and sprint up the mountains. In the wind, time
or season
slips my mind. Palm clenches
and loosens, an intertwined
destiny—I remember how I pulled through May
and made a promise under the stellar sky
I have returned . . . Again and again
in the backyard
I plant seeds, mistakes, love

白云栈道

"有雨山戴帽，无雨山没腰"
这话，确是一点都没错啊。住在白云山脚
观白云，占晴雨
渐渐地，使我获得一种力
混淆进任何我所在之处的背景中

我是一阵凉风里，消失的古寺
古寺里，凝固的钟声
是山腰处空心的松柏、飘忽的云雾
又是这儿几棵，那儿一片的野茶
被还原在清晨的光线里，无人再来认领

——不是我不愿将自己交出
沿栈道一路往上
山涧奔腾喧响，各种寂静试验着它们的宽广

The Gallery Road of White Clouds

In rain the mountain wears a hat, without rain its waist is doused with clouds
Living at the foot of Mount White Cloud
where clouds augur rain or shine
Mixed in the backdrop wherever I go
I've earned strength

I'm a vanishing old monastery in a gust of cool wind
Frozen chimes in the monastery
Mindless pines and cypresses, clouds and fog at the mountain waist
Wild tea trees here, another stretch there
back into morning light rays, never claimed

—not that I demur to hand myself in
Along the gallery road
mountain streams surge and resonate, each stillness testing its own width

挽留之殇怎堪说

在我年轻的岁月里，我曾是一颗行星么
夜空下，绕着你窗口的灯光默默辗转
直到露水浸湿了鞋帮
无法说清这是怎样的夜晚
但身体知道，那灯光，那恒星
那如同太阳光芒的灼伤

而今不惑将至，激情，仅来自于冒险，以及
与自身的对抗
人世的汪洋里，我波浪般
上下起伏，难以形容
那挣扎的躯体，多变的形式
到底标志着什么："遗忘"？还是"挽留"
或者，仅是一个十字

没有别的出路。我把自己扔得如此之远——在日常的
淡淡的顺序中，因为惶恐而获得了生命

How Can I Find Words to Grieve and Not Let Go

In my young days, was I a planet that tossed and turned
in silence, circling your window light under the night sky
until dew soaked your shoes
Hard to explain such a night
but my body knew the light, that fixed star
burns passing for the sun's luster

Soon forty, I've learned that passion stems from risk and one's
own antagonism
In this cosmos, this ocean, I undulate
like waves, beyond words
What does this struggling body, a metamorphic form
symbolize: *Oblivion? Or not letting go*
or just a crossroad

There is no other exit. I've thrown myself so far out—in the daily
dull order, I find life through terror

绿弦

五、六月，南方多雨。我辗转
变淡，成为简谱上
逐渐隐没的音符——那不曾诠释，或者
尚未诞生的……我明白
不论停留在哪儿，我都是
一个缺失。因此，这有生之年
我得满足于
自己的一颗心——满足于它的
偏执、狂欢、冥想、欲求不息……请缓缓开启
慢慢靠近——
慢慢地，在古筝的绿弦上，对应上四四拍
与D调音……

Green String

In May, June, the south has more rain. Tossing and turning
I pale, into notes
gradually hidden in simple notation—never once interpreted, or
yet unborn ... I know
no matter where I stop, I'm always
a defect. So, in this lifetime
I must be content
with my heart—content with its
bigotry, wild joys, meditations, endless desires ... Please unlock gently
slowly lean closer—
slowly, on a green harp string, in tune with 4/4 time
and D major ...

所在

一床、一椅、一桌、一盆萱——
去年九月，给它喝水之前，它枯萎，缩在墙角边
一扇窗户，紧贴着，岩石和潮湿
一间不断掉墙皮的屋子，打开门，那么多的蔓草
涌了进来……从院子里，山坡上
一座山。山下的
一条隧道，有时深夜，传出的歌声

Whereabouts

A bed, a chair, a table, a pot of orange daylilies—
last September, they withered before watering, shrunken in a corner
A window attached to rocks and humidity
A house with walls peeled, door open, a rush of weeds
creeping in . . . from the courtyard, on the hillside
A mountain. Down the mountain
a tunnel, sometimes echoes of singing late at night

重归莲花峰

星期一，搬回到山上。莲花峰
在暮色中，恢复着
本初的布景——风在林间，青苔在岩石上
只有流水
去了山的那一边……我清楚，这是
另一种生活
是我只身到来和离开的地方
那刮进窗户的
是去年秋天的味道

Back to Lotus Summit

Monday—moving back to the mountain. Lotus Summit
regains its composure
at twilight—wind in the woods, moss on rocks
Only water
has run to the mountainside ... I know this
is a different life
where I come and go alone
The taste of last autumn
sweeps in from the window

秋天深了

我早早地套上了毛衣
骑车到外面，尽量避开
两旁事物投下的阴影
洗澡的时候，我拉紧双层的浴帘
我在厨房做饭
把紧挨着山岩的窗户关上了
可还是有毛虫和蚯蚓
掉了进来。好像
它们也怕秋天，秋天
深了。有那么一刻我爬上屋后的山顶
整个地，藏身于暖阳之中——
而林子呜咽着，落叶，正一点一点
掉进我的身体……我知道
躲不过的，是即将来临的冬天，是雪

Autumn Deepens

I put on a sweater as soon as I can
Riding a bicycle, I avoid shadows
from both sides as far as possible
When I bathe, I pull tight the double shower curtain
I cook in the kitchen
shut windows next to rocks
But caterpillars and earthworms
still drop in, as if
they too fear autumn. Autumn
deepens. I reach the summit behind my house
The whole place, hidden within a warm sun—
groves sob, fallen leaves, dot by dot
dropping into my body . . . I know
I can't avoid winter, the coming snow

雨

持续多日，雨停留在莲花峰一带
雨衣在厨房里滴着水，窗外的草
长得有半人高了

但我不记得去过哪，在哗哗的响声里
我是多么地害怕
另一个人，从我身体里，径直走出……

Rain

For days it rains in the Lotus Summit
Raincoat dripping in the kitchen, grass outside
waist high

Yet I can't recall where I've been, in these loud torrents of rain
how I fear
someone else, walking out from my body . . .

西湖大道

我步入每天的生活
在斑马线上踯躅，依次经过
两岸咖啡、雷纳森名店、银行、毗邻的
超市和酒家。一只
蚂蚁，转遍了整个菜市场
也没找到合适的粮食

哦，下雨了。人们因这突如其来的冰凉而蹙眉
加快了步履。而折磨我的
却是另外一些，普通人类
小小的欲望

——无辜的欲望
落下来，散发出时间和泥土的气味
令我皱缩不已
这车水马龙的西湖大道
这大道上，失去了声音和形体的雨点

West Lake Avenue

I step into daily life
loiter on the zebra crossing. Passing by in succession
C-straits Café, Rinasaint luxury shop, bank, adjacent
supermarkets and restaurants. An
ant, spiraling over the food market,
finds no proper food

O, it's raining. In this rush of cold, people frown
and hasten their steps. But what tortures me
are other tiny, banal
human desires

—innocent desires
are falling, their scent of time and mud
wizens me
On this teeming West Lake Avenue
raindrops lose their voices and figures

杭州下雨了……

白堤上，那些桃树、柳树
和梧桐树
都湿了
一些闪亮的雨水，顺着
战栗的枝条
落进了湖水里
以及路中央，树木的
影子里……一颗颗
波动的心

沿着西湖，经过断桥，直至
小孤山，北风吹着
雨中的江南
吹着你，和我
在彼此呼出的热气里，我们也
渐渐地，变湿

Hangzhou Is Raining...

On the White Bank, peach trees, willows
and wutongs
are wet
Some sparkling raindrops, along
trembling branches
fall into the lake
and tree shadows at the center
of the street ... hearts
undulate one by one

Along West Lake, through the Broken Bridge, right till
Mount Xiaogu, north wind blows
at Jiangnan in the rain
blowing you and me
In our hot exhalations, we too
turn wet, finger by finger

一截土墙

疏松。大雨过后，阳光烘烤的气息
何首乌藤晃动
斑驳的光影
或者甬道。密布且隐秘的呼吸，细碎、涌动
使我缩小，充满
热烈的心跳

A Piece of Mud Wall

Loosening. After a downpour, the toasted smell of sunlight
Chinese knotweeds tremble
Motley shades and shadows
Or a corridor. To breathe densely in secret, fine pieces, a billowing
that shrinks me
in a hot heartbeat

巢穴

我更愿意独处。在这颗蓝色的星球上
在自我的深处，我仅有的
已经像这秋天的荒野
敞开。三十余年，辗转迁徙
置身其间的，是不尽的山陵、野甸、河流
是橘树、水杉、槭树、榆树、香樟、栗子树……
我愿意它们
就是我今生的朋友和亲人
而我，皱缩于任何一棵枝桠间
每一天，从草窝里探出黑豆般
惊怯的双眼：多么不可思议的世界
山高水长，树木荡漾
太阳升起了
太阳又要落下——时间已经
不多了。"事物只能是它自身"，那么，我也愿意

Nest

I'm more willing to embrace solitude. On this blue star
deep in myself, all that I have
opens up like autumn
wilderness. Moving around for over thirty years
in the midst of boundless hills, wild pastures, rivers
orange trees, water firs, maples, elms, camphor trees, chestnut trees . . .
I'm eager to have them
as friends and kin in this lifetime
I wrinkle up between twigs on a tree
Like black peas my panicked eyes pop out, every day
from a grass nest: what an incredible world
High mountains long rivers, rippling plants
The sun rises
and sets again—time
is running out. *Things are only of themselves,* let me also be

个人生活

我的大部分时间
都是和自己
呆在一起。以前
是四面群山中的一座庭院
现在则置身于
莲花峰上的一间屋宇，幽暗、低沉
日夜点着灯

每天，我试着与不同的自己
交谈
关于良知、道义、公平
关于信念、坚持、以及内心
莫明的恐惧……
但我不清楚，这其间
是否真的
就达成了某种共识？有时候
她是那么小，在鸟鸣和水声中变轻
有时却又是一座山的喧嚣
和沉寂

当我无话可说的时候，我会
起身，去推开屋后的那扇窗户
让她们看看
那照在山脊上的太阳，那一大片的
静止和响亮

Personal Life

Most of the time
I stick
with myself. In the past
among mountains in a courtyard
now within
a house on Lotus Summit, dim and gloomy
a lamp burning day and night

Every day, with my different selves I try
to converse
about conscience, morality, justice
about faith, perseverance, and an inner
odd fear . . .
Meanwhile, I can't tell—
have we reached
an agreement? She is sometimes
so tiny, weightless in bird calls and water sounds
Yet other times she is a mountain's clamor
and quiet

When I'm speechless, I will
get up, push open the window behind the house
let my various selves see
the sun on the ridge, that expanse
of still and echo

谵语

就这样吧，身为一颗尘埃
我从未抱怨过，自己的微小。同样地
我也不认可，这人世间
所谓的真理和至上的权威——如果连你
也感到遗憾，并失望，那就
轻轻地抹掉我。如同抹掉
我对这个世界最后的错觉

Delirium

So be it, as a grain of dust
I've never resented my slightness. Likewise
I disapprove of the so-called earthly
truth and supreme authority—if you
find it a pity, then just
whisk me away. Like wiping off
my last illusion

散步

先准备好钥匙
再预备一些钱，我总是不确定
每天的散步，我会走到哪里，我将去哪里
然后找出手机插进兜里。那上面
有我远方的亲人和朋友
倘若路上有不测，我想他们中的谁，也许会过来
会将我认领……

好了，现在，我是一个
可以随时回来，随时走远，随时死去的人了
留下一盏台灯在屋子里，亮着
我轻轻地带上了房门

Stroll

Keys first
or money, I can't make up my mind
A daily stroll, wherever I walk, wherever I'll go
then find my phone and pocket it, carrying
my distant kin and friends
In case of mishap, I imagine one of them coming
to claim me . . .

Alright, now, I'm someone who might
return anytime, who can travel far and die anytime
leaving behind a desk lamp, lit in the house
I softly close the door

More than Mountains:
Reading the Mystery in Ye Lijun

> Pine needles feel too soft under my feet
> My heart throbs
> I don't know how to walk
> to place myself safely in this mountain
> —"Chronicle of Mount White Cloud"

One of the more promising women poets of the "post-seventies" generation in China, Ye Lijun[1] was born in 1972 in Lishui, in the southern province of Zhejiang, to an impoverished family. Her father was a peasant, her mother a member of the pioneer generation of Chinese intellectual youths sent to the country for "labor re-education" at the outbreak of Mao's disastrous Cultural Revolution (1966-1976). Since a tender age, Ye Lijun developed a passion for painting and literature. Although she started writing during her high school years, she chose to pursue a professional life in the visual arts: after graduating from the Zhejiang Educational Institute for Professional Art Pedagogy in 1995, Ye found work as a junior high art teacher in Shuige ("Water Pavilion"), a small village town in her native city Lishui.

---

1   "Ye," which means "leaf," is the poet's family name, and "Lijun" her first name.

An aspiring painter from a rural background who had known poverty since childhood, Ye Lijun was largely on her own, removed from the cultural milieu and mainstream. Her teaching experience in Shuige proved to be mundane and dispiriting: it exposed her to the daily struggles of rural children, most of whom were deprived of books or basic schooling, let alone take an interest in artmaking. Ye soon grew disillusioned, both with her job and artistic impasse, and the larger socio-political setting. Originally a rustic southern hamlet, Shuige underwent different stages of economic reforms and industrialization that had rapidly affected its forestry, agriculture, and pastoral tradition. Lishui— literally translated as "Beautiful Water"—with its mountainous suburbs were no less vulnerable to frenzied patterns of urban changes and environmental problems still prevalent in other areas of the present-day China. Against a backdrop of a vanished wilderness and mutilated landscapes, in the wake of escalating privatization and social pressure to "succeed" or "prosper," Ye Lijun joined the growing middle class of her generation who had to confront the spiritual lack of a more worldly—but no longer sustainable—life:

A small town among mountains in the south
Four distinct seasons, a river loiters free
Dawn redwoods line each path, towering on both sides
In this small town, I teach at Shuige Junior High
A discarded classroom
A bed, a table, a chair
After my classes, I'm on my own

Ten whole years, I lead a simple life
So why change vocation? When people ask
I blush in shame and stammer
not knowing what to say
                              —"Memories of a Small Town"

Poetry has much to do with Ye Lijun's "change in vocation," as one learns from the above excerpt from one of her more personal lyrics. When Ye began to access the Internet in 2001, she was quickly drawn to the literary forums burgeoning online. By way of hasty generalization, one might say the turn of the twentieth-first century was a watershed for many Chinese writers and intellectuals, poets in particular; now over a decade after the 1989 Tian'an-men Massacre, several gradually felt assuaged of civil repression or self-censorship, thereby coming together to explore the virtual world as an outlet for dialogue, publication, or literary bonding. It was during this time that Ye rekindled her love for writing: she found in poetry solace and purpose, and more crucially, possibilities of expressing her conflicted inner/outer worlds. A self-taught poet, she began to study and write outside work seriously.

Unlike most of her peers, Ye Lijun sought translated literature very early in her poetic education. She read as much fiction and philosophy as poetry. Not surprisingly, her literary tastes seem more eclectic and "cosmopolitan" than of those from her generation and region: Sappho, Cavafy, Amichai, Pessoa, and James K. Baxter are Ye Lijun's all-time favorite poets, to name a few. Continual sources of inspiration include Kafka, Simone Weil,

Camus, Nabokov, Yasunari Kawabata, and Juan Ramón Jiménez. Novelists Kim Hoon, Jeanette Winterson, and Can Xue, as well as American poets Robert Penn Warren, James Wright, and Louise Glück are among her more contemporary preferences.

Through poetic creation, Ye re-interprets her world as a reader. She adopts techniques of intertexuality in some of her poems by appropriating or alluding to specific lines and characters. For example, she quotes from classical literature across all cultures: Tang poets Wei Ying-wu (737-791) and Po Chü-i (772-846)—both of whom exemplify ancient Chinese poetic heartstrings for the much-revered mountains and landscape—and among others the fourteenth-century Flemish mystic-writer, the Blessed John of Ruusbroec. Further, she makes direct reference to modern-day work by Carson McCullers and Jorge Luis Borges. Because of her deft intertexual cues, Ye Lijun's own language blends a contemporary feel with a voice reminiscent of classical verses. Such linguistic sophistry, in which music shapes intent and informs content, lends weight to the overall lyric texture, especially for poems with an unmistakable narrative impulse.

In others, Ye replays her reading life unveeringly by dramatizing scenes from books and juxtaposing them with elements of truth or actuality. One might come across colloquial fragments of her self-ramblings or a palimpsest of responses culled from assorted phone conversations and meetings. In a brief poem "Reading a Mora Novel at Night" for instance, Ye Lijun stages herself within a fictional scene by contemporary Hungarian-German woman writer Terézia Mora, and enacts a dialogue with a real lover who also exists as a "he" in Mora's

narrative. As a result, poetry functions as both mimesis and diegesis—the poem in itself becomes a site, theatrical and real, where multiple temporalities co-exist to perform divergent streams of consciousness:

> *Just forget it.* He curls up in an armchair
> and leans his body backward,
> *Like me when I forget to leave, forgetting myself here*
> *in this room.*
> Hands on the chair start to display
> a wooden color and texture. I rub my eyes
> O, deep night
> *To this end,* he continues,
> *most of us are stuck in life.*

In 2004, after almost a decade of teaching, Ye took unpaid leave from work and enrolled in a graduate program at China Academy of Art in Hangzhou. She specialized in oil painting. Now a wife and the mother of a six-year-old daughter, Ye used her own savings to carve out "a room of her own"—an austere life of painting and books, away from her hometown, family, and child—to be all by herself, in a rented place at Lotus Summit near the scenic West Lake. Yet, this period in her life was not just of quiet studies and re-adjustment, but also grief, doubt, and existential angst: two months before her move to Hangzhou, her brother died at age forty from a car accident. As if by bittersweet twists of irony, Ye began to achieve some literary renown that same year when her poem "Passing by Thousands

of City Lights in Black Night" was highlighted nationwide by *Poetry*, one of the top literary periodicals in mainland China. Sixteen of her poems appeared as a feature in a subsequent issue.

Steadily since, Ye Lijun has established herself as one of the representative southern lyrical poets whose writing finds a broad readership in influential literary journals including *People's Literature*. She has to her name several literary prizes and nominations, not to mention over five hundred publications across the nation, nearly a hundred widely anthologized. A debut collection *Survey* was released in 2005 by Dazhong Literature and Art Press in Beijing, followed by the second *Passing by Thousands of City Lights in Black Night* from Chongqing University Press in 2009. Both received critical acclaim. When her third and most recent volume, *Flower Complex*, came out in 2014 from Changjiang Literature and Art Press in Wuhan, Ye chose not to do readings or engage in any book publicity.

◊

Ye Lijun writes about the country, but she also writes about the city, and above all the various phases of her life that take place between the country and the city. A regular commuter between two of the most scenic cities in the south, Hangzhou and Lishui, Ye has in recent years spent brief stints in Beijing. Via frequent train journeys, the poet finds distance from her personal sphere of experience, and is made more aware of larger

transitions in life and landscape. Transposition from the country to the city (and vice versa) is visual—at times even cinematic—but it is the temporal shift that displaces poetic trajectory, thwarting expectations most dramatically. For example, in "A Broken Heart Takes the Night Train," while "[t]he train passes through Jinhua (a city in central Zhejiang) for a layover," the poet-traveler moves along with it into a dark tunnel: a painful past of brother-and-sisterhood that she has disconnected with for years now springs up—

> A range of black mountains and beanlike lamps
> An infinite landscape where here is elsewhere
> yet . . . Jinhua . . . out of the blue, a dust-
> sealed instant strikes
>
> Twenty years ago, Brother sent her off
> for her entrance exams in Jinhua. Penniless, they caught
> a random cargo truck
> and alighted in the suburbs
> Brother carried her drawing tools, took her hand
> and walked to town
> After rounds of instructions, he bid her farewell and set for home
>
> But she plunged headlong
> into her destiny—a whirlpool—never turned back
> or stopped to reflect . . .

At first read, the poem comes across as a straightforward narrative that involves flash-backs, regrets, melancholy, and pangs of

conscience. Yet there lies more than the work of retrospection: triggered by the forward and backward momentums of the train, the poet identifies with not just "a range of black mountains and beanlike lamps" outside the window, but the shift of consciousness that pivots on the continuity of landscape: "An infinite landscape where here is elsewhere." This continuity of landscape suggests timelessness, a lyric construct that exerts pressure on the narrative in which Ye the poet must now testify not just to the memory itself, but to the act of recalling and longing for this memory. Such longing is more explicitly disclosed—in first person, for example—when Ye metamorphoses into a tree in a self-portrait that honors the metaphor (the tree) above its subject (the poetic "I"):

> Although I can't go back in time, I may grow and multiply
> Each branch I extend
> will carry on these secrets:
> a heap of snow, paper slips, pills, kisses in the darkroom,
> > lonely camellias
> blossoming in my green brick house . . .
> > —"Tree"

In Ye Lijun's work—notably her place-specific pieces— the poetic "I" is often a lonely feminine figure in reflective mode, such that her solitude reinforces her conviction in fatalism, and provides an impetus for nature and the nonhuman to intervene, even if it might be no more than a fragment of memory within an urban mise-en-scène. After all, *[h]er travels*, the poet states in

"Partial Solar Eclipse," *can never transcend her selfhood*. And it is in Lishui, her native city where the poet returns unfailingly to mourn, heal, renew, and reconstruct. As in the case of British Romantic painter John Constable, who sees in the landscape that he was born with a lifelong emotional map for his art, Ye finds it impossible to separate herself from Lishui, whether in life or writing. "I should paint my own places best,"[2] remarks John Constable notably, after his failure with landscapes outside the Stour Valley in his birthplace of Suffolk.[3] Likewise for Ye who, in her own words, internalizes Lishui as alive and breathing in her "bloodstream," the poet feels most at home with its mountainous wild. More vitally, this lays the ground for Ye's ecological conscience, a visionary clarity that she would further deepen through poetry and the course of a lyric time-space. By interiorizing Lishui, she can "sing or speak" of the place "from authentic experience": *the sheer fact of being alive* with and within the landscape.[4] Such interconnection on the consciousness level is symbiotic, ineffable, raw, and sacred. For this reason, Ye seems at her best—tender and all-embracing—in nature poetry informed by vivid details and lush imagery from her hometown:

> … Moving around for over thirty years
> in the midst of boundless hills, wild pastures, rivers

2   See Pavord, Anna. *Landskipping*. London: Bloomsbury, 2016. 45 and 223. [Pavord cites the source for Constable's quotation: "John Constable, writing to Archdeacon John Fisher, 23 October 1821, in R. B. Beckett (ed.), *John Constable's Correspondence*, vol. VI (Ipswich, 1968).]
3   *Ibid*, "A Fitting Landscape," 45.
4   Snyder, Gary. "Poetry and the Primitive: Notes on Poetry as an Ecological Survival Technique." *The Ecological Conscience: Values for Survival*. Ed. Robert Disch. New Jersey: Prentice-Hall, 1970. 195.

orange trees, water firs, maples, elms, camphor trees,
                chestnut trees . . .
I'm eager to have them
as friends and kin in this lifetime
                                        — "Nest"

But it is not merely the picturesque and its tropical culture
that opens up her body/mind/soul, bonding or stretching her
poetic imagination with geography and the physical odds. On the
contrary, Ye Lijun continues to find inspiration in Lishui even
when nature and places from her country childhood have faced
threats of vanishment from rampant urbanization, tourism, local
policies, and climate changes. Gary Snyder reminds us, *[P]oets
don't sing about society, they sing about nature—even if the closest
they ever get to nature is their lady's queynt.*[5] That Ye's response to
Lishui tends to be elegiac is, on the other hand, hardly a surprise;
in "Autumn Deepens" she writes, "I reach the summit behind my
house / The whole place, hidden within a warm sun— / groves
sob, fallen leaves, dot by dot / dropping into my body . . . I know
/ I can't avoid winter, the coming snow." In spite of it all, the fact
that her strong attachment to the place and mountains begins
almost always with wonder—a sense of marvel—bears witness
to her psychic surrender to their scope, an artist's humility and
gladness before their mystery, and her enduring faith in nature,
both its self-restorative prowess and cosmic command. Despite
its poverty, geophysical isolation, scarce infrastructure, and lack
of social polish, Lishui is where the poet returns to seek the roots
of her existence, literally and literarily. She never takes its wild

5   *Ibid*, 198.

lands for granted. Mountains transcend mountains because they embed a cosmos, an intelligence, a music and silence that she poetically interprets as "memory" and "spirit" on the whole—that of the earth, beasts, and mankind, prehistoric or present. These are presages of the wide-ranging mythical encounters on which Ye would meditate before immortalizing in verses:

> Quiet all around, summits green and bright, I sat on a stream rock
> listened to grass and trees endure the jointing stage in silence
> and indifference

> until one noon, after some urgent whistles
> a red-billed blue magpie
> appeared atop the horizon, its long
> white feather like a phoenix tail, elegant and calm, resting
> at the valley
> in an azure sky . . . O this solitary soar
> these mountain country years, the secret bestowal . . .
> —"My Mountain Country"

In Ye Lijun's poems, readers can trace two distinct maps, each featuring an inviting list of local haunts and sites in Lishui and Hangzhou. These comprise less a checklist of popular destinations than a private archive of addresses and niches the poet holds close to heart over the years: Mount White Cloud, Pingyi Village, Ping'er Village, Pingsan Village, Lake Sky, River Ou, Lake Dayang, West Lake, Lotus Summit . . . Conscious or not, Ye Lijun is enacting a scientific practice dating from the Renaissance.

As American environmental essayist Paul Gruchow describes it, "One way to understand our relationship with nature is to undertake the basic work of naming its constituents."[6] The way she has taken to naming places, as well as plants and animals encountered during her mountain strolls and outings creates in her poems an immediate sense of real that compels us to inhabit Ye's environs, seasonal walks, and ambulant imagination. It is edifying for an outsider to catch a glimpse of these places not just because they sound mostly foreign, far, and atemporal, but that they play a significant role in mythologizing the poet's lyric narratives and themes.

Recurring on the page, in particular, is the image of a green brick house, which Ye Lijun baptizes affectionately as "my country green house." In 2008, Ye bought a humble green stone house in the countryside of Lishui near River Ou, and until 2011, spent almost all her weekends at this retreat where she could write, read, meditate in isolation, and akin to a hermit, lead a non-consumerist lifestyle à la Thoreau. One gets the sense that by then, city life was taking its toll on the poet who needed refuge and repose. In quest of an alternative pace, a less exploitative culture, and a more primitive modus vivendi, Ye was in search of a different voice and thought.

For the poet, the location of this green brick house is emblematic: it is situated at the village end of the River Ou, with an uplifting view of its meanders. To live by the River Ou—the second longest river running through Zhejiang Province—is a symbolic return to her birthplace. In one of her longer free-verse poems "Hymn to the Spring Water," Ye Lijun writes:

6   Gruchow, Paul. "Naming What We Love." *Grass Roots: The Universe of Home*. Minneapolis: Milkweed Editions, 1995. 124.

> . . . Before my eyes lies the growling River Ou
> All the way, over hills and valleys
> it sprawls through here, turns and swirls, suffused with a fatal
> fishy stench, indifferent to fame or gain
> I know its secret source: in southwestern Mount Donggong,
>   a wetland
> pushes aside messy dead weeds

At her country green house, the poet eats what she grows, studies herbology, and picks up stargazing. Here, she becomes attuned to an eco-friendly life and takes a keen interest in local biodiversity, specifically the interactions of flora and fauna, and their sensory effects on human language or drama. In the opening poem of this volume, "Sitting and Waiting for Daybreak," the poet acknowledges the forceful synergy of the encircling flora and fauna by bowing down to the silencing interplay of the woods, crickets, trees, little beasts, and bees: "I just / hug myself, sit in this dim, wobbly center / listen with breath held, until // this world sounds its highest scale / —dawn, stillness. And I choose / to utter no word."

Ye refers nostalgically to these years as her "green house period," and does not cease to revisit them in poetry. It makes reference to a crucial time that nourishes Ye's spiritual and creative development: during this period, her poems grow in strength, while as a citizen, she is made more and more environmentally mindful by the progressive fragility of her surrounding ecosystem. Since 2011, her village has weathered different chaotic construction projects, some unplanned. Nevertheless, it has become increasingly difficult—physically and emotionally—for Ye

to visit her green house, especially after the illegal construction of a new six-storey building by the river, and consequently, the view from her green house entirely blocked and destroyed, the riverscape partially refashioned but no longer durable.

◊

I have evoked mystery and its presence as an approach to Ye Lijun's work, and it calls to mind how one of my literary heroes, French poet René Char (1907-1988) has been drawn to mystery throughout his life, and prominently as the philosophical arc of his major work, *Fureur et mystère* (*Fury and Mystery*, 1948). One of Char's English translators, Robert Baker, makes an astute observation in an introductory essay for his recent translation of Char:

> Char has many names and figures for the mystery that poetry brings to light in words. Sometimes he calls it the open, or the summit, or the upland, or the unknown. At times he figures it as the transparence of dawn, akin to the divine dawn that Rimbaud pursues in one of the simplest of his *Illuminations*. Elsewhere he imagines it as the clarity of a night within the night, beyond the night, akin to the 'cool transparent night' that Whitman is drawn to.[7]

I can say the same for Ye Lijun's poetry, though in her case, the mystery is more of a metaphysical appeal, an abstract archetype.

7   Baker, Robert. "René Char: The Hermetic Boundary between the Shadow and the Light." *The World as Archipelago* by René Char. Richmond, California: Omnidawn, 2012. xiii.

This, again, seems to call for the substance of poetry as untouchable or beyond human reach. Ye intuits the mystery in a self-imposed solitude—for instance, her weekly retreat to the green house—or via the "movement" she "found deep down" during a visit to "the canyon nearby" when "[i]n spring, all things on earth share the pain of fission" ("My Mountain Country"). A Westerner might be quick to criticize the romanticism of solitude and such hermetic lifestyle as a new-age trend, but we must consider the prevailing contexts of Chinese politics and culture: solitude and retreat are rare efforts in the current "neo-Communist" China where the collective is privileged over the individual, while the latter is conditioned to being generic. Other than in monastic communities, projects that champion living alone in spartan conditions—moreover, for reasons of well-being—are unheard of, even unimaginable, for the greater Chinese mass who still struggle with survival and fantasize about owning a car, a refrigerator, and a television. Far from being clichés, solitude and an eco-friendly life distant from the mainstream are uphill endeavors for a mere person—furthermore a woman—in an overwhelming crowded and paternalistic nation of more than one point three billion where life is cheap, its carbon cycle hijacked and clean air politicized.

Mystery also comes to Ye Lijun in darker manifestations such as "motley shades and shadows" ("A Piece of Mud Wall"), ruins ("a house with walls peeled," from the poem "Whereabouts") or ungainly sights ("so many / blacks ants / that couldn't be buried, outpouring in the backyard / from a fluffy cave," from the poem "Backyard"). Oftentimes, Ye honors the mystery with speechlessness, expressing it in terms of ellipses or em dashes.

She, too, avoids inserting periods or commas at the end of verses. The mystery is invisible yet audible, which we can see in images such as "the secret heart of an alarm clock" in "Thus Have I Heard," or even immortal such as stars "set apart by billions of light years" in "A Starry Night Education." For Ye Lijun, mountains are the all-encompassing holders of this mystery, so in this respect, the poet herself is within and part of this bounteous mystery. De facto, Ye learns to tame herself before this elusive but ubiquitous mystery so that her breath and body embody it, such that the poetic self gains at once depth and ephemerality:

> Living at the foot of Mount White Cloud
> where clouds augur rain or shine
> Mixed in the backdrop wherever I go
> I've earned strength
>
> I'm a vanishing old monastery in a gust of cool wind
> —"The Gallery Road of White Clouds"

The word *mystery* fuels the birth of many worlds and languages, as well as the disappearance of boundaries. During a conversation with world-renowned field biologist Edward O. Wilson, American poet Robert Hass evokes Wallace Stevens, who "in one of his last poems says he imagines as a kind of final act of nature a bird singing 'without human meaning, without human feeling, a foreign song.'" Hass adds, "The idea that every creature has its own reality scared poets ... made some of them feel we were groping blindly—it in effect kicked us out of a

comfortable anthropocentric community—but it also allowed some modern poets this sense of absolute mystery at the core of existence."[8] I believe Hass is referencing Stevens's classic "Not Ideas about the Thing but the Thing Itself," in which the old poet questions himself about "a scrawny cry" he heard as first "a sound in his mind" before it came to him as "part of the colossal sun," a concreteness, a sound and an existence free of imagination or order.[9] This is powerful poetic realization whereby the artist imposes upon himself an alertness, a lucidity that dissettles—and in turn exiles—imagination with a capital "I" from the invisibles that define reality. Ye Lijun's poems shelter such mystery because they underscore experience over thought by honoring the unsayable and the unknowable, even if the poet has reversedly, or unconsciously, attributed them to her human shortcomings— her lack of knowledge, control, or words—and a physical unease with her own body:

> my rigidity and dullness
> signs on my body suffering from corrosion
> wait to be fondled, to be pierced
> wait to open in clarity, leading to this specific instant
> and you. Roused at night, eyes wide open, I lie with fear
> >   in darkness
> all invisibles fade in a rush
>
> . . .

8   Wilson, Edward O. and Hass, Robert. *The Poetic Species: A Conversation with Edward O. Wilson and Robert Hass.* New York: Bellevue Literary Press, 2014. 55.

9   Stevens, Wallace. "Not Ideas about the Thing but the Thing Itself." *The Collected Poems of Wallace Stevens.* New York: Knopf, 2008. 534.

I cluster leaves
I awaken roses
Just like this, I possess what I don't
An imaginary troop
        — "The Secret Hour"

The idea of being uncomfortable with one's own body is in fact an erotic one. It invites an outsider's gaze or imagination to resolve psychic tension and complete the delayed carthasis. At the core, it is about revealment and concealment. In several of her love poems, Ye Lijun's poetic "I" tends to expose her unease with her own feminine body at the same time she strips it naked, while concealing the identity of "you" the lover/onlooker. She downplays the state of being desired in order to prolong the desiring. In poems that are openly sexual, expressly "The Secret Hour," "Naked Spring," "In Search of Porcelain," and "Within the Reach of My Memory," the mix of uncertainty and self-consciousness mutates gradually into anticipation, irresistibility, sensual pleasure, and hunger. Love is edible in Ye Lijun's poetry: in one of her best-known poems "Flower Complex" and a shorter lyric "Brew," we learn that the poet cooks and eats flowers, as well as brews "three kinds of wine." Love is a season brought to fruition and renewal. The fact that lush, colorful metaphors of nature prescribe many of Ye's love—and most intimate—poems seems to allude to the inevitability of all great nature poetry: *love* (verb), *love* (noun), and *love* (adjective).

◊

I have been translating Ye Lijun since 2011. This bilingual volume compiles sixty-six poems from all three of her collections: *Survey* (2005), *Passing by Thousands of City Lights in Black Night* (2009), and *Flower Complex* (2014). They are, in our view, poems representative of Ye's writing life over the past fifteen years. Instead of arranging them by order of chronology, the poet and I have decided to sequence the poems with an outline more authentic to their emotional authority, artistic truth, and narrative arc: the first section "Song of Tremble" sets the stage for Ye Lijun's green house and mountain days, as well as her various inner landscapes when she approaches middle-age. The intermediate "Partial Solar Eclipse"—a metaphor of sorts for a lapse in memory and plot—includes texts that relate to the poet's family and personal past, situations, and travels, testifying to time as abyss and bridge (or in-between the two) in myriad ways: several of these poems might each be what Milosz considers as a *poem-epiphany*, a *moment-event*,[10] and an eloquent revelation somehow or somewhere. The last part "In Search of Porcelain" returns to Ye's growing sense of spiritual ecology and revivifies her previous lives spent in a mountain hut (which one may decode as either the green house in Lishui or her earlier dwelling on Lotus Summit in Hangzhou—or creatively, a mythologized blend of both). In short, each section lays claim to its own time-integrity and flow, and the collection as a whole. Translation at its most sustainable is at heart a mystery. I hope my versions of Ye Lijun keep alive the mystery in her poetry as much as that of the act of translating.

Fiona Sze-Lorrain

---

10   Milosz, Czeslaw. *A Book of Luminous Things: An International Anthology of Poetry*. San Diego, New York, and London: Harcourt Brace & Company, 1996. 3.

NOTES

I. SONG OF TREMBLE

Hymn to the Spring Water
The source of the Ou River (Zhejiang Province) is in the
Guomaojian Wetland in southwestern Mount Donggong.

Bathing in the Open at Zhaitou
Zhaitou is a village in Songyang County, Zhejiang Province.

II. PARTIAL SOLAR ECLIPSE

Grass-things
In Chinese, each item, name, title, or place specified in
this poem—Grass Tower, cursive, tiger lily, grass carp, *The
Pillow Book*, grass hut, *Essays in Idleness*, "Herborist" skin
products, the Herbal Heaven shop, and Asakusa—contains
the character *cao* ("grass"), which is why the poet refers to
them as "grass-things."

The verse "[A]lone, I savor wildflowers tucked in along
the creek" is from Tang poet Wei Ying-wu's poem "At
West Creek in Ch'u-chou," translated by David Hinton in
Mountain Home: The Wilderness Poetry of Ancient China
(London: Anvil Press Poetry, 2007).

Waiting or Et Cetera
Published in 1975 in an eponymous collection of short
fiction, "The Book of Sand" ("El libro de arena") is a short
story by Argentine writer Jorge Luis Borges.

Reading a Mora Novel at Night
Born in 1971 in Sopron, Hungary, Terézia Mora is an
acclaimed German-language woman novelist, screenwriter,
playwright, and literary translator.

In the Study Late at Night
The quotation [*God is the sea, the billows, the ebb and
flow*] is from the Blessed John of Ruusbroec (1293-1381),
a Flemish mystic whose writings include *The Spiritual
Espousals* and *The Sparkling Stone.*

A Sent-Down Youth Is Back in Town
A sent-down youth, also known as a *zhiqing*, refers to an
urban youth sent to the country for re-education and labor
during the Cultural Revolution.

III. IN SEARCH OF PORCELAIN

In Search of Porcelain
In one of China's four great classical novels, *Dream of the
Red Chamber* (1791), mud and water are metaphors for a
man and woman.

Wind Goes On
The italicized words in lines 7 and 8 are from the poem
"Inviting Liu Shih-Chiu" by Tang poet Po Chü-i (772-846),
translated by David Hinton in *The Selected Poems of Po
Chü-i* (New York: New Directions, 1999).

Up the Mountain
The quotation is from the title of Carson McCullers's first
novel, *The Heart Is a Lonely Hunter* (1940).

ACKNOWLEDGMENTS

Heartfelt gratitude to the editors of these journals in which several of the poems/translations were first published: *Antigonish Review, Chattahoochee Review, The Literary Review, New Poetry in Translation, Poetry London, Poetry Northwest,* and *Salamander.*

Fiona Sze-Lorrain also wishes to thank Bai Hua, Christina Cook, Natasha Sajé, Alyson Waters, and Donald Nicholson-Smith for their invaluable assistance and wisdom.

The award-winning Chinese contemporary poet YE
LIJUN was born in 1972 in Lishui, Zhejiang Province to
an impoverished rural family. A graduate of the Zhejiang
Educational Institute for Professional Art Pedagogy and
China Academy of Art, she worked as a junior high art
teacher and arts administrator for intangible cultural
heritage. The author of three poetry titles—*Survey* (2005),
Passing by Thousands of City Lights in Black Night (2009),
and *Flower Complex* (2014)—Ye has received several
literary honors in China, including the 2007 "Poetry Tour"
Award. Currently, she resides in her native city Lishui and
serves as an editor at *Lishui Literature*.

FIONA SZE-LORRAIN is the author of three books of
poetry, most recently *The Ruined Elegance* (Princeton,
2016). A zheng harpist and widely published translator, she
lives in Paris where she works as an editor. She was named
the 2019-20 Abigail R. Cohen Fellow at the Columbia
Institute for Ideas and Imagination.

The English text of *My Mountain Country* is set in Garamond Premier Pro, and the Chinese text is set in STKaiti. Cover photograph: *A Thousand Metamorphoses of Souls* (1929) by Kōyō Okada (1895-1972). Cover design by Kyle G. Hunter.

MY MOUNTAIN COUNTRY